Photo credits:

Doug Perrine/Innerspace Visions: Pages 8,11-15,24,26
Gwen Lowe/Innerspace Visions: Pages 6,18
Rudie Kuiter/Innerspace Visions: Pages 18,19,24
Norbert Wu/Innerspace Visions: Pages 14,19
Mark Conlin/Innerspace Visions: Pages 15,29
Michael Nolan/Innerspace Visions: Page 8
Ron & Valerie Taylor/Innerspace Visions: Page 13
Nigel Marsh/Innerspace Visions: Page 15
David B. Fleetham/Innerspace Visions: Page 19
Amos Nachoum/Innerspace Visions: Page 20
Tom Campbell/Innerspace Visions: Page 23
Scott Michael/Innerspace Visions: Page 25
Jeff Rotman/Innerspace Visions: Page 28
Norbert Wu: Pages 6-7,12,21,27-29
Bruce Rasner/Norbert Wu: Page 22
Marty Snyderman: Pages 7,22,25,26,28
Doug Perrine/DRK: Pages 7,13,19-21,29
Stephen J. Krasemann/DRK: Page 27
CC Lockwood/DRK: Page 27
Flip Nicklin/Minden Pictures: Pages 7,10
Stephen Frink/WaterHouse: Pages 10,21
Robert Jureit/WaterHouse: Page 11
Ron & Valerie Taylor/WaterHouse: Pages 11,13,21
Marty Snyderman/WaterHouse: Page 29
Al Giddings/Images Unlimited: Page 6
Rosemary Chastney/Images Unlimited: Page 9
David J. Wrobel/Biological Photo Services: Pages 9,14,27
Harold W. Pratt/Biological Photo Services: Page 23
Bruce Elliot Rasner: Page 27
Wayne & Karen Brown: Page 28
David Hall: Page 11
Al Grotell: Page 18
Richard Hermann: Page 25
Marilyn Kazmers/SharkSong: Page 27
Jim Watt/Pacific Stock: Page 23
Don Flescher/American Fisheries Society: Page 9
Gotshall/American Fisheries Society: Pages 24,26

Illustration: Robin Lee Makowski - End pages; Pages 16-17,19

Front Cover: James D. Watt/WaterHouse
upper left: David J. Wrobel
upper right: F.S. Persico
lower left: Doug Perrine/DRK

Copyright © 1995
Kidsbooks, Inc.
3535 West Peterson Ave.
Chicago, IL 60659

Manufactured in the United States of America

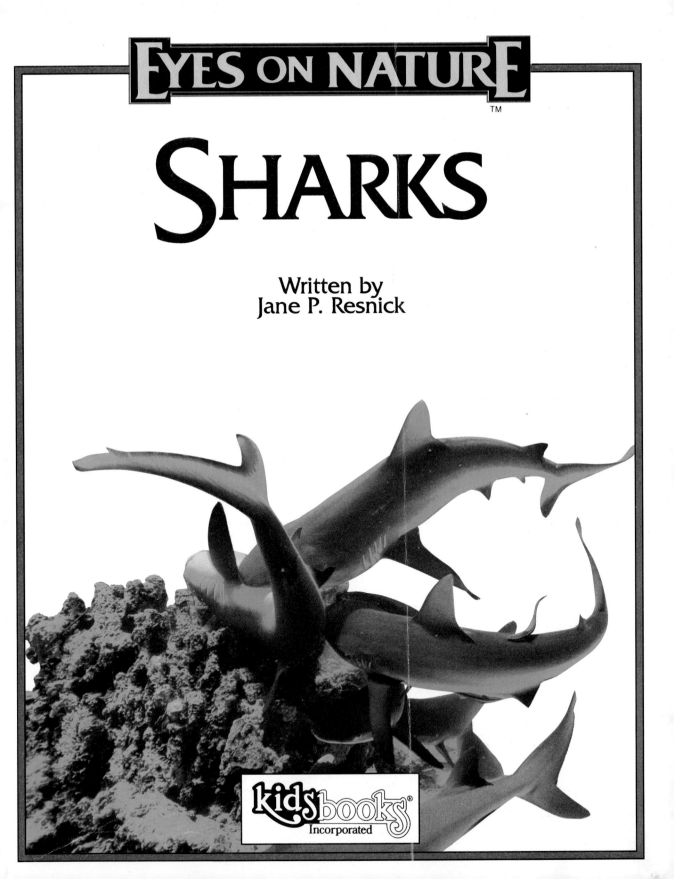

EYES ON NATURE ™

SHARKS

Written by
Jane P. Resnick

kidsbooks ®
Incorporated

SHARK!

Terrifying, magnificent, mysterious—sharks are masters of the sea. They're real survivors, built so well that in the last 150 million years, they've had very little need to change, or *evolve*. And, in some form or another, they've been around for about 400 million years. Even before dinosaurs roamed the land, sharks ruled the oceans.

Pygmy shark

FAMILY MATTERS

Sharks belong to the group of fish known scientifically as *elasmobranchs* (e-LAS-ma-branks)—a big family. There are over 350 species, and they are very different from one another. Some are large, but most are fairly small. In fact, only 39 species are over 10 feet long. The largest is the whale shark (as big as a whale), and the smallest is the six-inch spined pygmy shark.

TELLTALE TEETH

How do we know there were ancient sharks? Their teeth have survived. Teeth are the best clues to shark evolution that we have. Although entire bodies of some sharks were found in the 19th century, usually it's the teeth, or even the scales, that have been preserved. Fossil teeth tell us about sharks that existed millions of years ago—and where the oceans used to be.

TIME OUT ▶

People used to believe that sharks never sleep. That's not true. Scientists have observed more and more sharks taking time out to rest on the bottom of the ocean. Nurse sharks sleep in piles of up to 40 members.

SENIOR CITIZEN

No one knows how long a shark lives. For example, scientists think the spiny dogfish shark may live for 30 years or for 100. To make a better guess, scientists now tag sharks in the wild and mark their spine with a chemical. The bones of a shark's spine have growth rings, just like a tree, which form through time. Scientists can later count the rings formed since the marking and guess a shark's age.

Bull shark

Whale
shark

MEAT EATERS ▼

Almost all sharks are *carnivores*, or meat-eating animals. They eat other fish, even other sharks, and sea mammals like dolphins and seals. Some feed at the surface on *plankton*—a mixture of plants and shrimp-like creatures. Then, there are the bottom-dwelling sharks, which feed on *crustaceans* (such as crabs) and *mollusks* (such as clams), crunching them with specialized teeth.

A blue shark feeding on mackerel.

WORLD
▲ TRAVELERS

Sharks live all over the ocean, in cold to temperate waters—usually cooler than 90° F. Some live in shallow waters, while others live in the deep and on the ocean floor. Some, like the blue shark, *migrate*, or travel, thousands of miles. And some species, the bull shark in particular, can even swim from saltwater into freshwater. Bull sharks have been found in the Mississippi River.

BUILT TO LAST

Sharks used to be called "living fossils" because they seemed so primitive. However, the more scientists study sharks, the more they believe sharks are complex animals. In fact, sharks may be one of nature's best designs.

BONELESS

Most fish have skeletons of bone and are called bony fishes. A shark skeleton is different. It's made of *cartilage*—the same kind of material as the human ear and nose. Shark cartilage is not as hard as bone, but it is tough and flexible.

HANDS OFF ▲

The skin of most fish has scales, but shark scales are different. Called *denticles*, shark scales are constructed like teeth—very hard, sharp teeth. Shark skin is like a spiky suit of armor. You can be injured just by touching a shark.

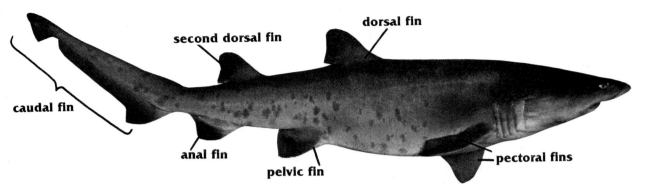

second dorsal fin

dorsal fin

caudal fin

anal fin

pelvic fin

pectoral fins

CRUISERS

A shark swims like no other fish. It doesn't flap and wiggle through the water. It glides. Its pectoral fins are stiff and are used for going up and down. The caudal fin is moved from side to side to propel the shark forward. Although some sharks can go fast enough to leap out of the water, sharks aren't built to swim fast all the time. Sharks are built to cruise slowly for long distances.

This shark has seven gills.

GILLS GALORE ▲

All fish use gills to breathe. Water passes into their mouth and out over the gills, which absorb the oxygen from the water into the fish's bloodstream. Unlike most fish, which have only a single pair of gill slits, sharks have five to seven pairs.

SINK OR SWIM

Most fish have a swim bladder that fills with air to keep them afloat when they're not swimming. A shark doesn't. It has to keep swimming to keep from sinking. But the shark has at least one flotation device—a big liver. The liver, which is sometimes a quarter of the shark's weight, contains oil. Since oil is lighter than water, it helps keep the shark afloat.

HOT BLOODS

Sharks are cold blooded, which means that their blood changes temperature as the water changes. But some sharks—the great white, the threshers, the salmon, the porbeagle, and two kinds of mako sharks—are known as "warm-bodied." They have a special heating system, so their blood is usually warmer than that of other sharks.

Great white shark

CRUNCH

The jaws of a shark are the most powerful on Earth. Both upper and lower jaws move. To bite, a shark strikes with its lower jaw first, then the upper. It flings its head from side to side to tear loose a piece of meat.

SUPERSHARP SENSES

A shark can hear, smell, and feel everything in the water—at great distances. With these supersharp senses, the shark has an excellent design for hunting. A school of fish may be passing through, or a fish may be hurt. The shark knows the difference and it reacts quickly, zooming toward its prey with deadly accuracy.

The nictitating membrane of a blue shark partially covering the eye.

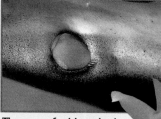

The eye of a blue shark completely covered by the nictitating membrane.

SMART SHARK

Sharks are often thought of as "swimming noses"—that they only use their brain to smell out food. Some, however, are fairly smart and can learn. Generally, the more active, fast-moving sharks have brains that are more complex than those of slower, bottom-dwelling sharks.

BLINK

Most fish have no eyelids, but some sharks have three—an upper, a lower, and a second lower lid. This second lower lid, called a *nictitating membrane*, can clamp shut and protect the whole eye in dangerous situations—like when the shark feeds.

GOOD VIBRATIONS

A shark can hear movement in the water, but it can also feel the vibrations by using its *lateral line*. This is a line of canals that runs from head to tail, linked to the surface of the shark by pores. Each canal is filled with seawater and contains special sensory cells with hairlike projections. These hairs move with vibrations in the water and then send messages to the shark's brain.

SWIMMING NOSE

Sharks do have a good sense of smell. In that sense, they *are* swimming noses! Two-thirds of a shark's brain controls its sense of smell. The two nostrils on a shark's snout are full of cells that detect odors in the water. In one experiment, sharks smelled a small bit of tuna from 75 feet away—smelling one-part tuna juice to a million-and-a-half parts water.

Blue shark

▼ ELECTRIC DIRECTION

All creatures have an electrical field. A shark "feels" this electrical activity with sensory organs called *ampullae of Lorenzini*. Leading to these organs are many pores, sometimes over 1,500 on the shark's head. Using its ampullae, a shark can find flat fish hiding under the sand. Because the Earth, too, has a magnetic field, it is thought that sharks may use this sense as a compass as well.

Lemon shark

Some sharks, like this lemon shark, have a vertically slit pupil.

NIGHT SIGHT

What do cats and sharks have in common? Their eyes. Both have eyes with a mirror-like layer that reflects light. This physical trait allows them to see better in the dark. So, whether in clear water or murky seas, a shark can still hunt.

11

A BITE TO EAT

The mako shark has long, narrow, pointed teeth.

Rows of serrated, or saw-like, teeth in the jaw of a tiger shark.

Think of sharks and you think of sharp, pointed teeth. But there are many different kinds of teeth. Shark teeth are so unique that scientists can identify sharks by them—or by the bite they leave behind.

DENTAL PLAN

Sharks have a lifetime supply of teeth—rows and rows set in soft tissue. An adult probably goes through 7 to 12 sets in one year. Each time a tooth is lost, by biting or through aging, a new tooth moves forward and takes its place. Some sharks, like the cookiecutter, swallow whole sets of teeth at one time when eating.

IN SHAPE FOR EATING ▲

Sharks do not chew. They swallow things whole or in big pieces. Some use their teeth like a fork and knife—they have pointed teeth in the lower jaw to puncture prey, and *serrated* teeth in the top to saw away at meat. But teeth vary from shark to shark, because the shape of a shark's tooth is related to the type of food it eats and the way it hunts.

A great white tooth on top of a Megalodon tooth.

TOOTH TALE

Scientists have found the teeth of a creature they call the Megalodon, an ancestor of the great white shark. It lived about 12,000 years ago, and it was *huge*. Its teeth were six inches long—more than twice the size of a great white's teeth.

ON THE MENU

Eating to survive is the name of the game in the ocean, and sharks are the champs. Some eat plankton, and some eat mollusks and crustaceans (like snails and shrimp) at the bottom of the ocean. Then there are those that eat larger prey, such as seals, turtles, seagulls, and dolphins.

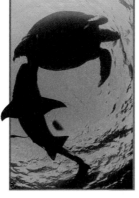

▲ A shark feeding on a turtle.

▲ The Port Jackson shark has sharp teeth in front for puncturing, and large molars in back for crunching the shells of mollusks.

Tiger shark

SHARK EAT SHARK

Sharks don't just eat other sea creatures. They also eat each other. Once, a tiger shark was caught with a bull shark in its stomach. In the bull shark's belly, scientists found a blacktip shark. And the blacktip's stomach revealed a dogfish shark!

FEEDING FRENZY

Normally, sharks dine alone. But sometimes they have a vicious party—a feeding frenzy. One feeding shark may attract others. Racing to the scene, they slash at the prey and bite wildly at anything that gets in their way—even each other. Then, it's over as quickly as it began.

SPECIAL DELIVERY

There are three ways that sharks begin life. They hatch from eggs outside their mother's body, the way chickens do. They hatch from eggs within the mother and are then born. Or, like people, their mother gives birth to them. Sharks have from 1 to 100 babies at a time, depending on the way they reproduce. The ones that give birth to a fully developed shark have fewer babies at a time than sharks that lay eggs outside their body.

A lemon shark is born!

BORN AT LAST

Sharks that are born, instead of hatched, grow inside the mother in much the same way human babies do. However, it can take sharks longer than nine months to finish developing. The spiny dogfish is pregnant for almost two years with her pups.

▲ The newborn lemon shark and mother.

◀ Dogfish shark embryo

Cat shark egg cases

THAT'S AN EGG?

Shark eggs are not "egg-shaped" like chicken eggs. They are tough, leathery, and rectangular, or shaped like spirals and screws. As the baby shark develops inside this *egg case*, it feeds on the yolk part like chickens do. In 8 to 14 months, a shark is fully developed right down to its teeth.

▶

Cat shark embryo and yolk

(1)

(2)

(3)

Full-grown
sandtiger shark

CANNIBAL BABY▲

A female sandtiger shark carries eggs that hatch inside its body. It produces many eggs, but the first to hatch is likely to be the only one born. This baby eats its underdeveloped brothers and sisters. That's how it grows—and grows. When it's born, the baby is about 40% the size of its mother—that's almost half.

THE GOOD MOTHER

Although sharks do not care for their babies after they have come into the world, mothers will search out safe places, called *nurseries*, where they can lay eggs or give

A pile of the spiral-shaped egg cases of the Port Jackson shark.

birth. The Port Jackson shark mother seems especially attentive to finding a safe place for her eggs. Scientists think that she carries them around in her mouth after laying them, looking for a reef crevice in which to lodge them for safe hatching.

A swell shark emerges from its egg case and swims off to live on its own (1-4).

(4)

TOUGH PUPS

A baby shark is called a *pup*, but it doesn't lead a dog's life. Its mother doesn't feed it or give it hunting lessons. In fact, grown sharks are happy to make a meal of tender babies. To survive, many young sharks go close to shore to grow up on their own. There are small fish to feed on there and no large sharks around.

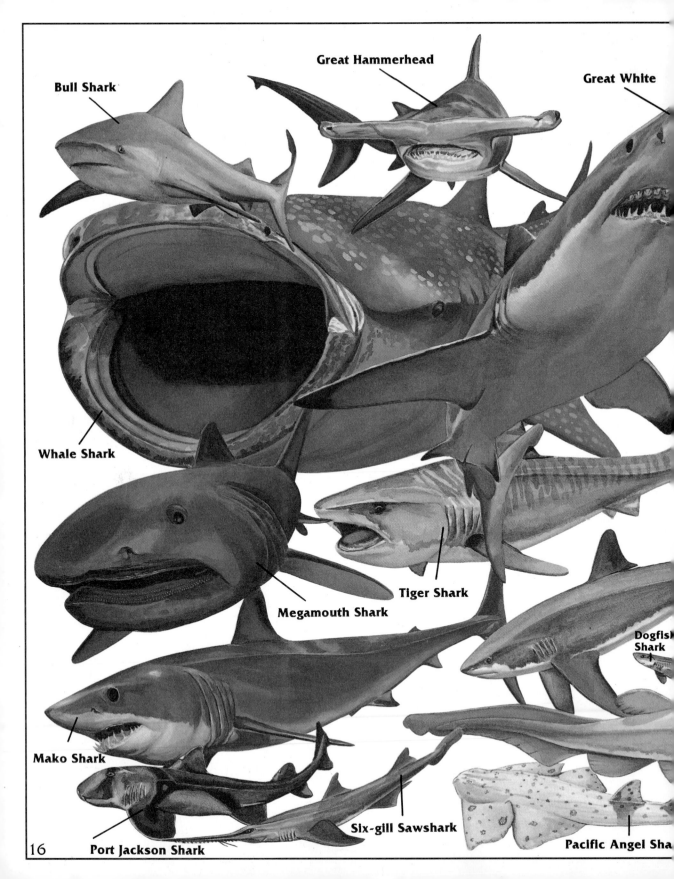

Great Hammerhead

Bull Shark

Great White

Whale Shark

Megamouth Shark

Tiger Shark

Dogfish Shark

Mako Shark

Port Jackson Shark

Six-gill Sawshark

Pacific Angel Shark

16

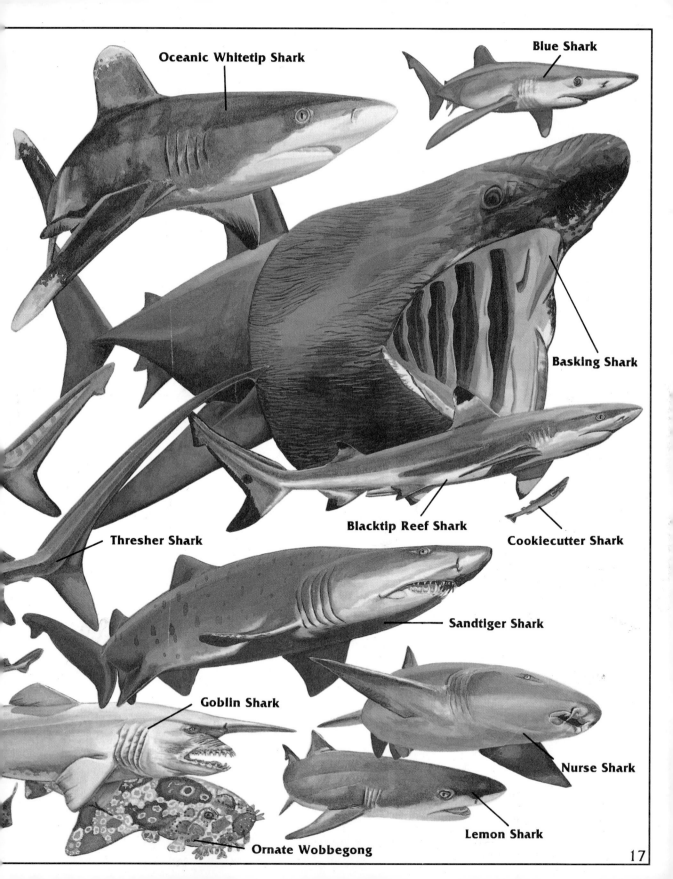

Oceanic Whitetip Shark

Blue Shark

Basking Shark

Thresher Shark

Blacktip Reef Shark

Cookiecutter Shark

Sandtiger Shark

Goblin Shark

Nurse Shark

Lemon Shark

Ornate Wobbegong

17

WEIRD RELATIONS

All sharks are hard to get to know. They have such a large living space that often they can't be found. Some sharks are rarely seen at all, and some are so weird to look at that, when you see them, you may not think they're sharks. In fact, one thing that is easy to see is how different sharks are—especially in the way they look.

Scalloped hammerheads are known to school when they migrate (above).

▲ Smooth hammerhead

HAMMER JAMMER ▲

Having eyes and nostrils some-times a yard apart, a hammerhead shark is able to sample a wide range of water at one time, sniffing out food as it swings its head from left to right. And, as if one weird head were not enough, there are many types of hammerheads.

◄ ANCIENT EATER

The frilled shark is often called "primitive" because it closely resem-bles some extinct species—some types of sharks that have disappeared from the Earth. The frilled shark has a slithery, snake-like body and 300 teeth set in 27 rows.

◄ HUNTING TAIL

The thresher shark has a 10-foot tail—that's about half as long as its body. This shark herds small fish together and hits them—whack—with its tail. Threshers are thought to be harmless to humans, but there is a story about one fisherman in the Atlantic who lost his head when swiped by a thresher's tail.

18

▼ COOL CATS

Cat sharks live mostly in deep waters and are rarely seen. They are one of the largest shark groups and live all over the ocean. But very little is known about them.

▲ SPOOKY

Maybe it's the strangest-looking shark of all, and, because it lives in deep water, it's almost never seen! Until found off the coast of Japan in 1898, the goblin shark was believed to be extinct for 100 million years.

IN THE TANK ▲

Some sharks are so gentle, they can be kept in aquariums. The zebra shark, also known as the leopard shark, is very gentle. It's spotted like a leopard, and its tail is half its length.

Cookiecutter shark

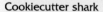

A dolphin with a cookiecutter wound.

CRUNCH

The cookiecutter shark is a 20-inch-long creature that feeds on whales and dolphins. With its circular set of teeth, the cookiecutter chomps a perfectly round hole out of its victim. Its teeth are so sharp, it has damaged rubber-covered parts of submarines.

Zebra bullhead shark

OLD TIMER ▲

Bullhead sharks are the oldest unchanged sharks. Fossils of them have been found in rocks 200 million years old.

19

DANGER!

Here's the nightmare: You see a fin and then a giant shark grabs you and crushes you with its teeth. Wake up! It's probably a dream. Here are the facts. Worldwide, fewer than 100 people are attacked in an average year by sharks. Some of these cases are provoked attacks, where the shark is caught, trapped, speared, or somehow bothered by people.

The most dangerous shark, the great white is known to chase down boats and attack them until they sink.

THE GREATEST

The great white shark is one of the largest, most deadly predators. Credited with more attacks on humans than any other shark, it grows to be about 11 1/2 feet and 7,000 pounds. Twenty-foot great whites have also been reported! It's the only shark that will lift its head above water.

TIGER OF THE SEA

The tiger shark is second only to the great white in the number of attacks on people. There is very little in the sea that the tiger shark doesn't eat. Some have been found with a few weird objects in their bellies—such as boat cushions, unopened cans of salmon, an alarm clock, tar paper, and a keg of nails! ▶

The great hammerhead is sometimes found in water only 3-feet deep.

Mako shark

SWORD SWALLOWER

The mako is powerful and thought to be dangerous. It is the fastest shark of all, clocked at 43 miles per hour. It is known to leap out of water—sometimes into boats! Also, the mako seems to have very little fear. A large, 730-pound mako was once caught with a 120-pound swordfish in its stomach—sword and all!

Bull shark

HAMMER HORROR

Seeing a hammerhead in the water might be enough to scare a swimmer to death, but scientists don't think that hammerheads are man-eaters. However, they consider a few kinds, like the great hammerhead and the smooth hammerhead, to be potentially dangerous because of their size.

KNACK FOR ATTACK

About 27 kinds of sharks are known to have attacked humans, and there are others considered dangerous. Shark attacks usually occur where there are a lot of people—in fairly warm, waist-deep water. It's possible that all the vibrations in the water resemble those of a wounded fish—a favorite shark meal. Attacks also occur where people are fishing.

◀ The blacktip reef shark is dangerous.

▲ BRUTAL BULL

The bull shark doesn't look as frightening as the great white, but it is in some ways more dangerous—certainly in the tropics. Listed as the third-most dangerous man-eater, the bull shark swims in places that people do—in salt water and fresh water.

NO-TEAR WEAR

People have tried over and over again to come up with chemical products and special diving suits that will repel sharks. One kind of suit found to help protect divers against bites is made of steel mesh.

Tiger shark

A diver wearing a steel-mesh suit while feeding a shark.

HUGE AND HARMLESS

Sharks are not always fierce and aggressive. Some sharks are harmless. And, strangely enough, the most harmless sharks are huge. These two characteristics, which do not seem to go together, belong to the basking shark, whale shark, and megamouth shark. They are the gentle giants of the shark family.

WHALE SHARK

The whale shark is the biggest fish in the world. Only about 100 have ever been seen. One captured near Pakistan in 1949 measured 41 1/2 feet long and was estimated to weigh 33,000 pounds.

ALL ABOARD

Believe it or not, whale sharks are so harmless, they let divers hold on to their fins for a ride. One diver says the feeling is like clinging to an underwater freight train. When whale sharks become tired of their human passengers, they dive deep into the sea.

◀ BIG SURPRISE

About 20 years ago, a navy ship off Hawaii accidentally hauled in a type of shark that had never before been discovered. It weighed over 6,000 pounds. Scientists gave it a name to fit its face: megamouth. It was another harmless, giant shark.

▲ SUNBATHERS

A basking shark can usually grow to be 30 feet long and 8,000 pounds. This fish is a mammoth sunbather. Its name comes from its habit of lying motionless in surface waters with its back above the surface and its nose and fins sticking out—as if it were "basking" in the sun.

▼ THROAT STRAIN

These huge, plankton-eating sharks feed by keeping their mouth open while swimming forward. Whatever comes in is strained from the water by *gill rakers* at the back of their throat. After awhile they swallow their catch. A cruising basking shark can strain about 2,000 gallons of water an hour.

A whale shark feeding.

▼ MINI-FOOD

Plankton is the diet of these big sharks. *Copepods*—barely visible lobster and shrimp-like creatures—are a large part of plankton. Scientists figure that sharks eat about 1% of their body's weight each day. For an 8,000-pound basking shark, that's a lot of plankton.

Copepods

The whale shark—the biggest fish in the world.

THE DEEP

What's more mysterious than the deep blue sea? The sharks that live there. There are many different types of bottom-dwelling sharks, and a few of them are really strange-looking. Some eat mussels, clams, and snails. Others prey on the swimming creatures that share their home at the bottom of the ocean.

A nurse shark exploring a reef. ▼

DEVILISH ANGEL

It's flat like its relative, the skate, but it swims like a shark, powered by its oar-like tail fin. It is a shark, an angel shark, but it's not an angel! Although the angel lounges motionless on the bottom, it has a swift and deadly bite, having sharp, dagger-like teeth for impaling fish and crustaceans. Fishermen who have tangled with it call it the "sand devil."

◀ SAWTOOTH

Here's one shark with teeth on the outside of its mouth. It's the sawshark. It has a long, flat, blade-like snout with teeth on either side, like a saw. Unborn sawsharks keep their teeth folded back until birth, protecting the mothers who carry them inside their body.

The face of a horn shark.

KILLER CARPET

To lie in wait on the ocean floor is the carpet shark's hunting plan. And no wonder! Carpet sharks have markings that blend in with the sand and a head that looks like a mop of weeds. No one sees it! Any fish that comes by is quickly snatched.

This creature, a kind of carpet shark called a Wobbegong (WOB-e-gong), is found in waters around Australia and the Far East.

HORN BACK ▲

This strange-looking bottom dweller, called the horn shark, can be found in shallow waters, too. Why is it called the horn shark? If you look closely at its dorsal fin, you can see a little horn at the front. People make jewelry out of these pretty fin spines.

Chain dogfish shark

A DOG OF A FISH

Spiny dogfish, smooth dogfish, spotted dogfish, chain dogfish—dogfish sharks are a large, varied family and their names prove it. In the 1400's, people with little knowledge of the sea gave them the "dog" tag. They called the sharks sea dogs or dog fish simply because these sharks have sharp teeth.

HOW SWELL! ▼

The swell shark is a lazy-bones, deep-bottom fish. It is so sluggish that it's called "sleepy Joe." But when threatened, this shark swells up by gulping air, until the center of its body is nearly twice its normal size. Why? Perhaps for defense, or to wedge itself into a tight hiding place. Both are swell ideas!

25

FLAT-FINNED KIN

▲ Adapted to lying on the bottom of the ocean, rays get fresh water to their gill chambers through a hole, called a *spiracle*, behind each eye. Note the spiracle on this bat ray.

Rays are the shark's closest relatives, for they, too, have skeletons made of cartilage. The rays are quite graceful, gliding through the water with pectoral fins shaped like wings. With a flat body, these fish have eyes on top of their head, a mouth and gills on the bottom, and a nose at the forward tip.

▲ At one-and-a-half-tons, with a fin span of 20 feet, the manta ray is no small relation of the shark's.

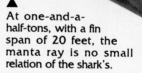

SUPER SCOOP

A manta ray streaks through the water with two fleshy parts that stick out of its pectoral fins like horns. These horns act like scoops, channeling fish, plankton, and other food into the manta's great mouth.

26

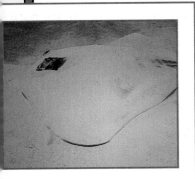

RAYS ROUND THE WORLD

Lurking in coastal waters around the world, are more than 100 kinds of stingrays. Some grow very large, weighing well over 600 pounds, sometimes with a fin span of more than 10 feet.

▲ A blue-spotted stingray found in the Red Sea, close to Egypt.

SHOCK EFFECT ▼

Some rays can deliver high-powered electrical shocks. One of these electric rays is called the torpedo ray. When it feeds, it swoops around small fish and shellfish, wrapping its pectoral fins around them and delivering a shock of 200 volts or more.

▲ A bullseye stingray found off the coast of Mexico.

◄EGG PURSE

The egg cases of a skate are often found on the beach. These cases are little black rectangles with strings. Long ago, people who found them thought they were left by mermaids. Even today, the skate's egg cases are called *"mermaid's purses."*

▼ SEE SAW

It's easy to see how the *sawfish,* another member of the ray family, got its name. It has a sawlike snout with razor-sharp teeth on the outside. By simply thrashing its head from side to side through a school of fish, the sawfish gets plenty of food for dinner.

Sawfish

◄ WATER SKATE

What's that shadow gliding along the ocean floor? It's a skate—an animal belonging to a large branch of the ray family. It's shaped like a kite, and its fins seem to ripple as it swims. Eating fish, snails, and clams at the bottom of the sea, the skate can grow up to six and a half feet long and weigh up to 100 pounds.

SHARKS AND PEOPLE

The shark is often used as a symbol for things that are frightening or dangerous. But, through studying them, scientists have learned enough about sharks not to think of them simply as killing machines. In fact, people are more dangerous to sharks than sharks are to people. We hunt them, pollute their water, and cause them injury, sometimes depleting whole populations.

Many sharks, like this dogfish, get caught in people's fishing nets and die. ◀

The jaw of this blue shark was probably torn by a fishing line or net, which are known to injure sharks and other sea creatures.

TREASURED TEETH

Shark teeth have been treasured for hundreds of years. People used to use fossilized teeth as charms to ward off evil and protect against poisoning. Pacific Islanders used shark teeth to make weapons (left). Today, people make jewelry out of shark teeth.

SKIN DEEP

People have hunted sharks for their skin for centuries. Sharkskin is 100% stronger than cowhide. It's used like any other leather, to make products such as shoes, belts, and purses.

MAIN COURSE

Shark steak or shark's fin soup on the menu? It's true. Soup is made from the fibers within a shark's fins, and shark meat is cooked like any other fish. In the United States, mako is sold all over. But in many countries shark steak may appear on the menu under a different name. The piked dogfish is known as "rock salmon" in Britain and as "flake" in Australia.

A mako shark caught by a fisherman.

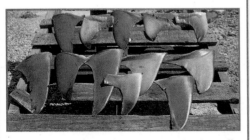

Unfortunately, some fishermen cut the fins off a shark for shark's fin soup, then throw the rest of the shark, still alive, back in the water to die.

TO YOUR HEALTH

Shark's livers were an important source of vitamin A until the 1950's, when scientists learned how to make this vitamin. Now, sharks are important to human health in other ways: Shark cartilage contains a chemical that is used to make skin for burn victims; and shark corneas have been successfully transplanted into human eyes.

◀ To study aging, these scientists are injecting a tiger shark with medicine that will mark the growth rings in its backbone.

▼ These scientists are working on a project to capture, test, and tag sharks.

STUDY BUDDY

Scientists also study sharks just to find out more about them, but it's not easy. When you can locate them, in the vast open sea, they're not always doing the things that you want to find out about, such as giving birth, schooling, or sleeping. But scientists have come up with procedures, like tagging and tracking, to get to know sharks better.

Here, a scientist studies the flow of water through a nurse shark's breathing system. ▼